This Book Belongs To

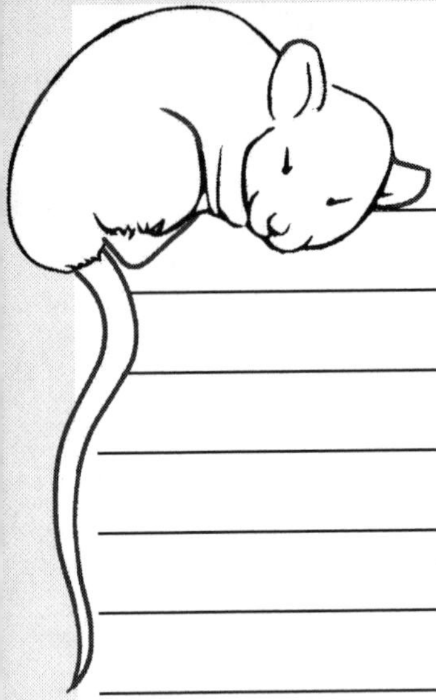

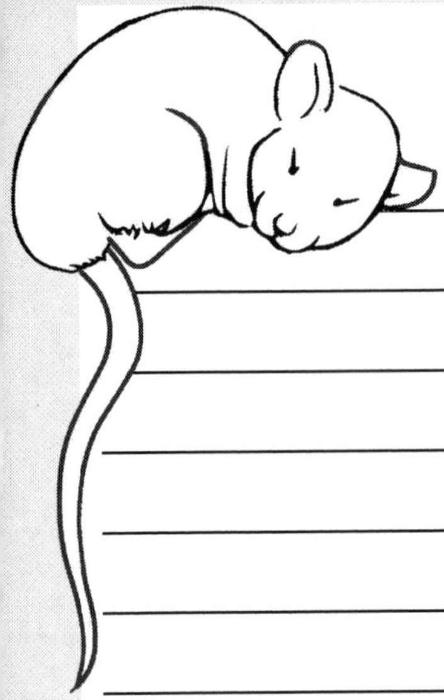

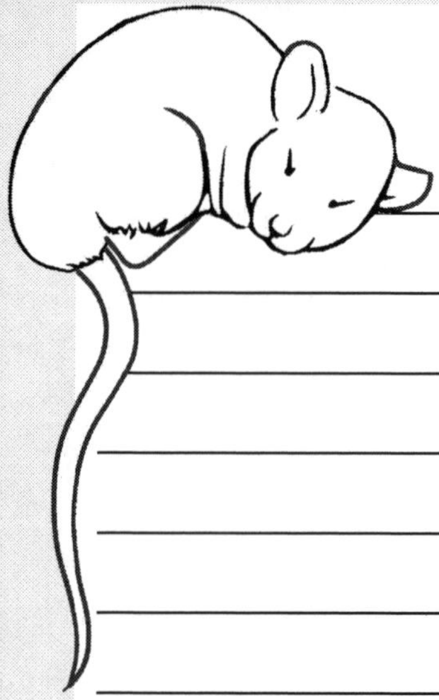

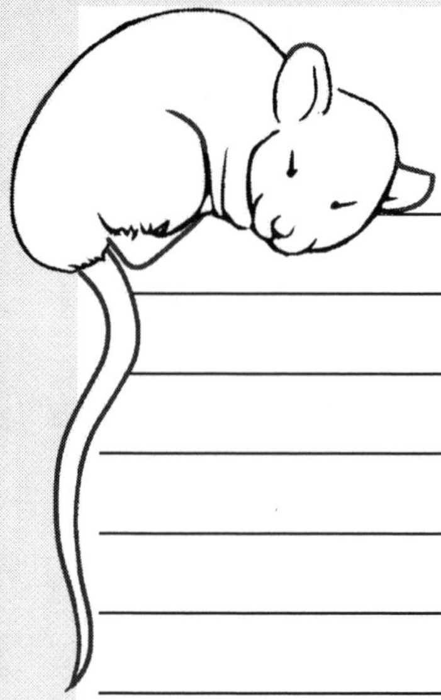

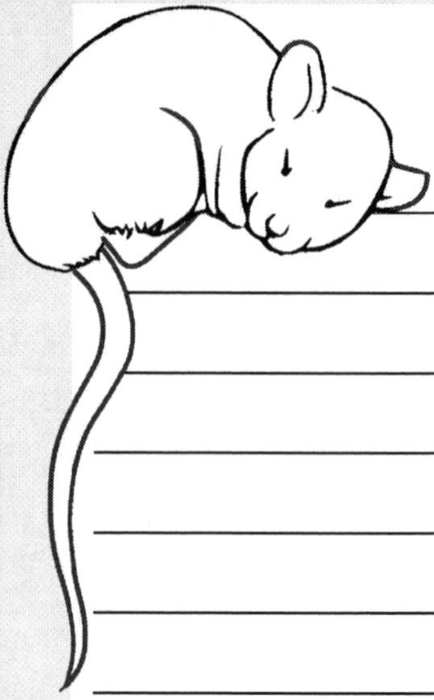

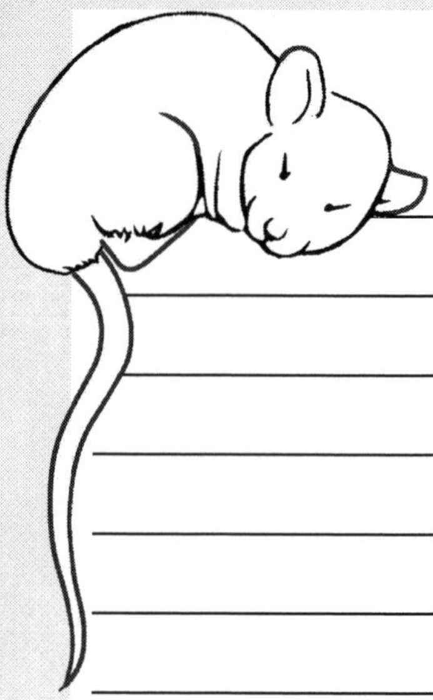

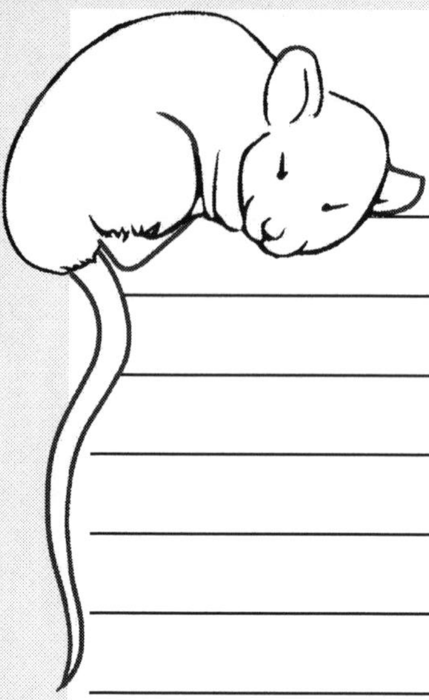

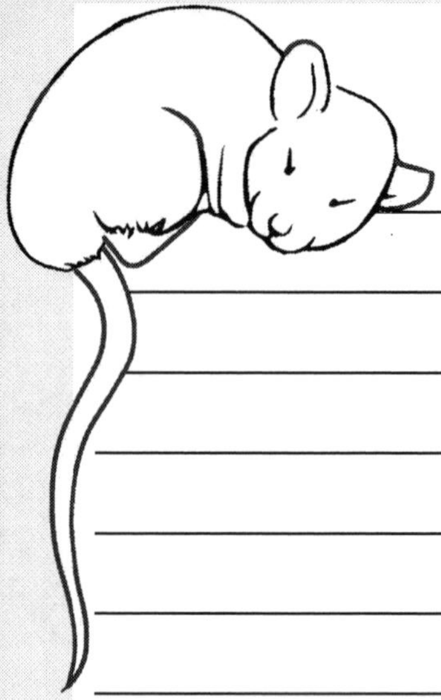

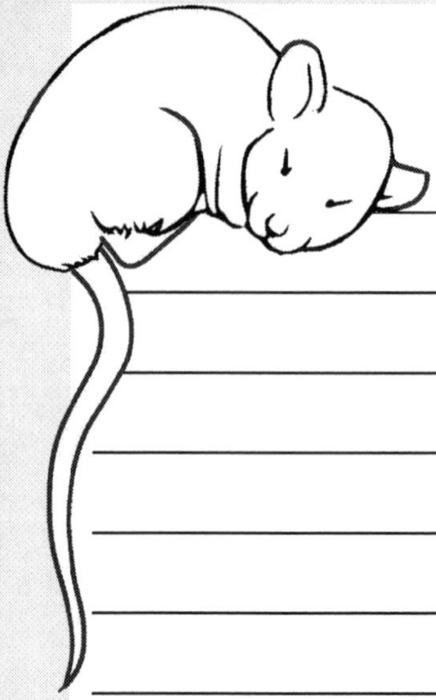

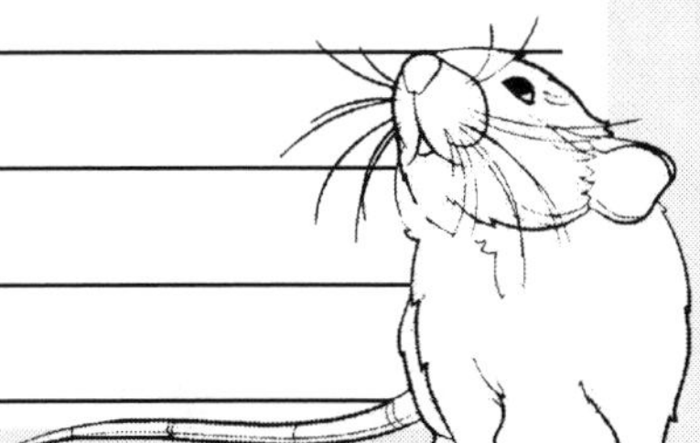

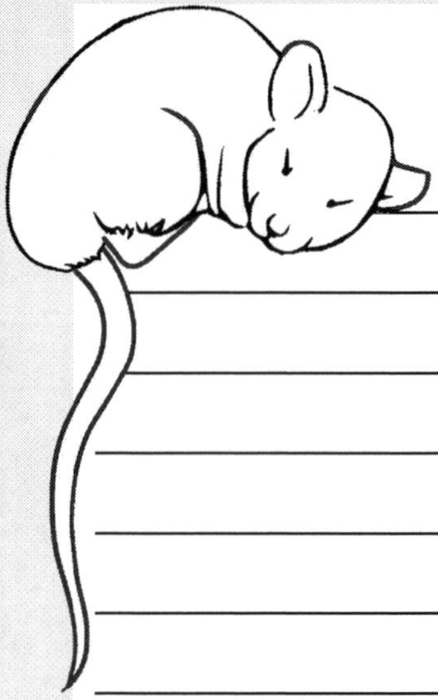

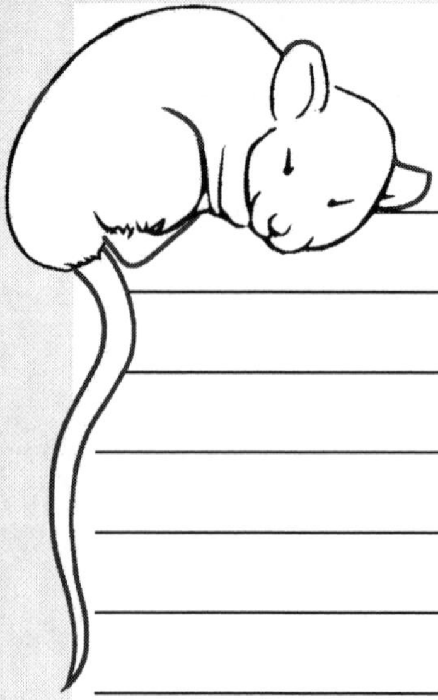

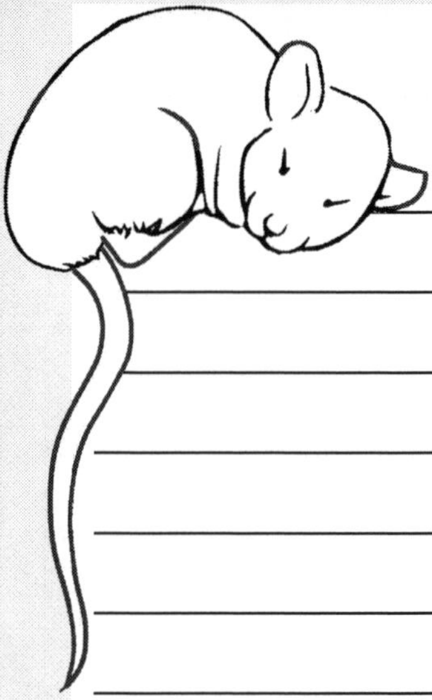

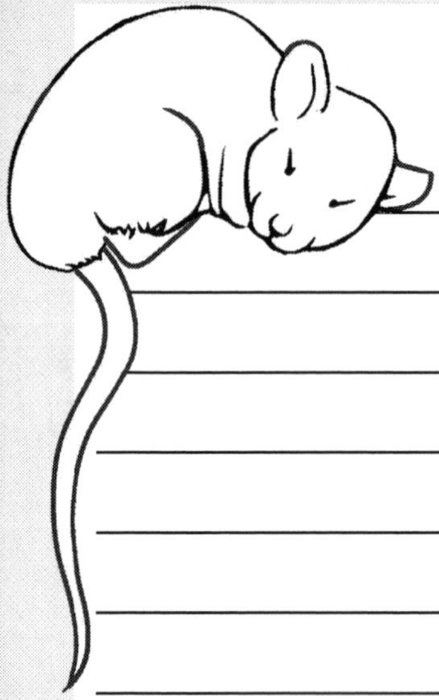

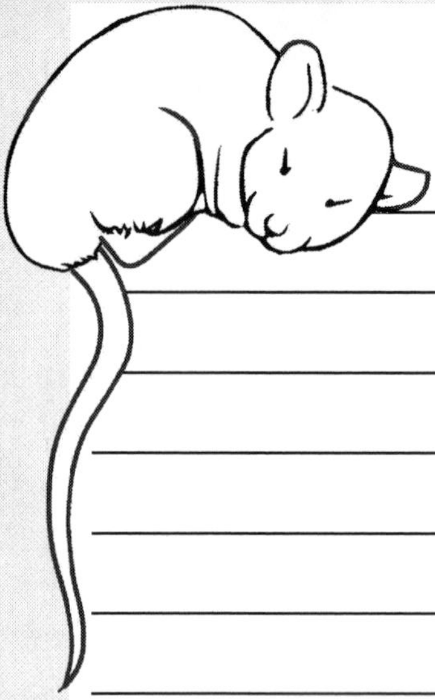

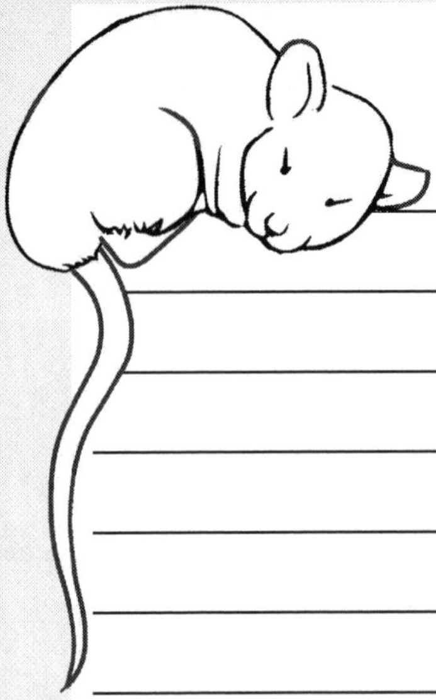

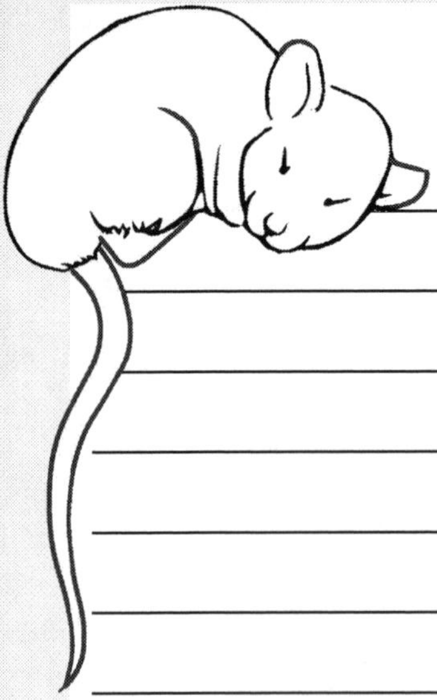

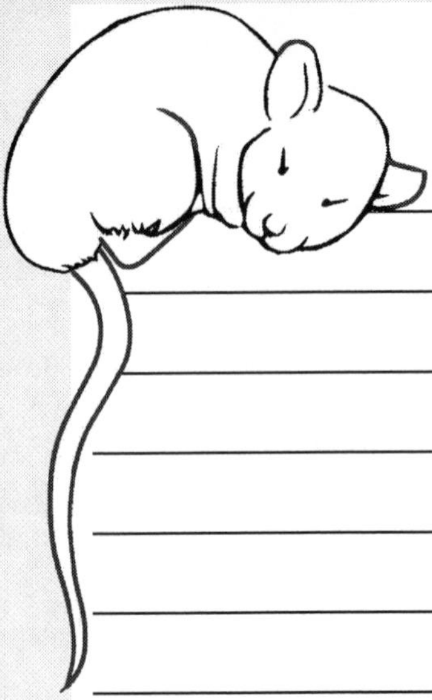

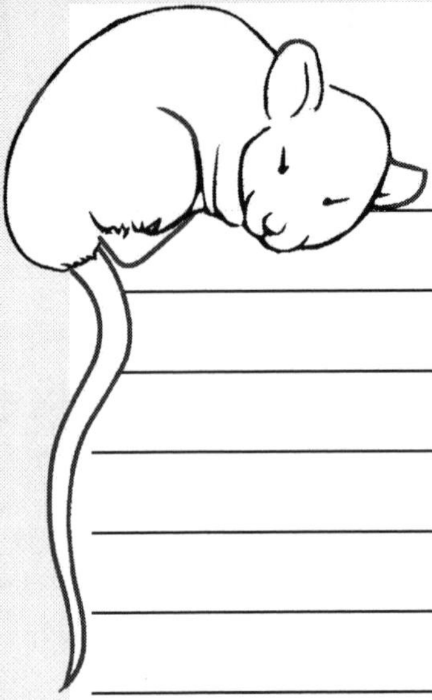

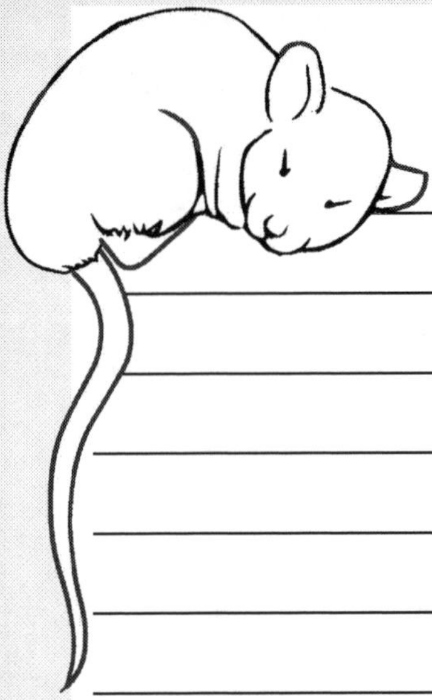

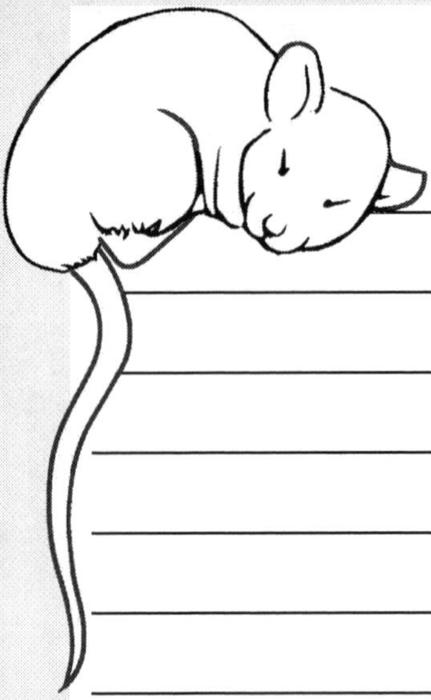

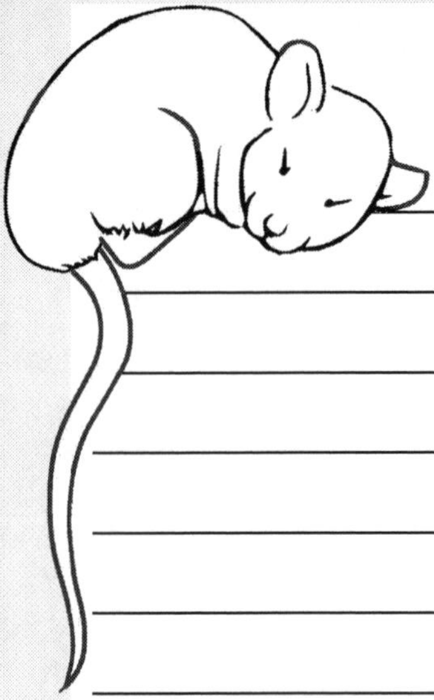

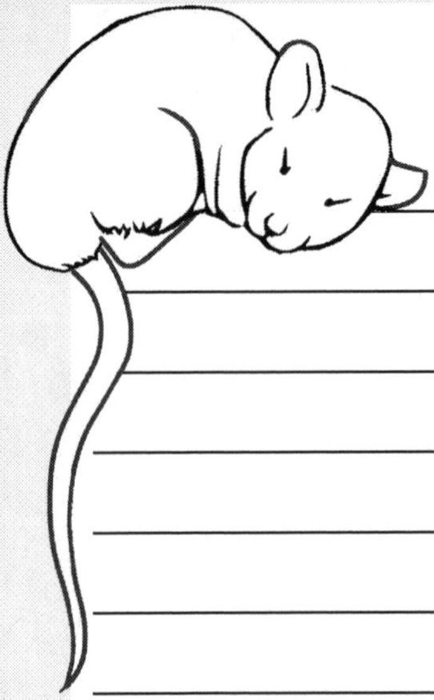

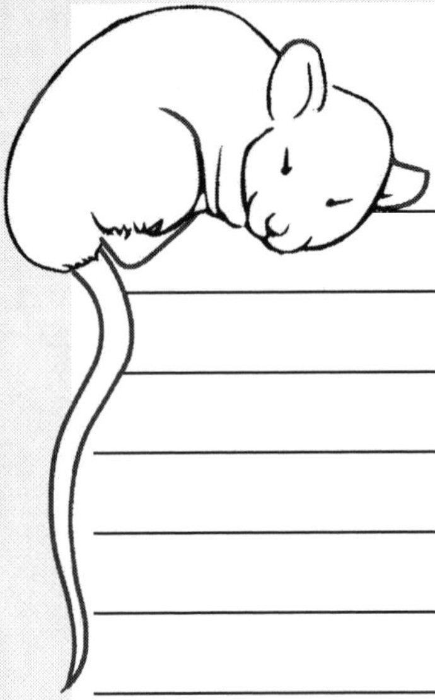

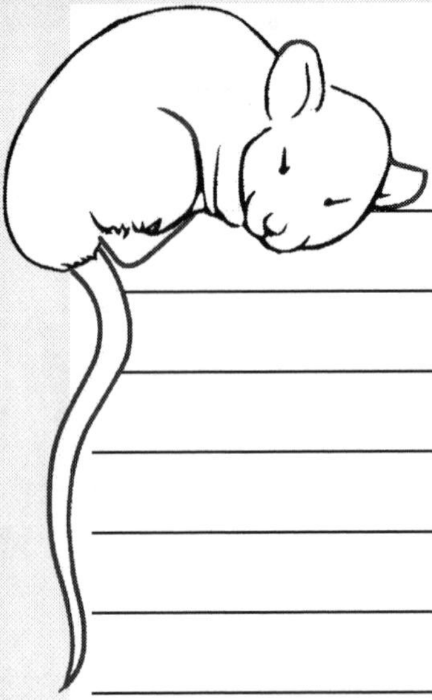

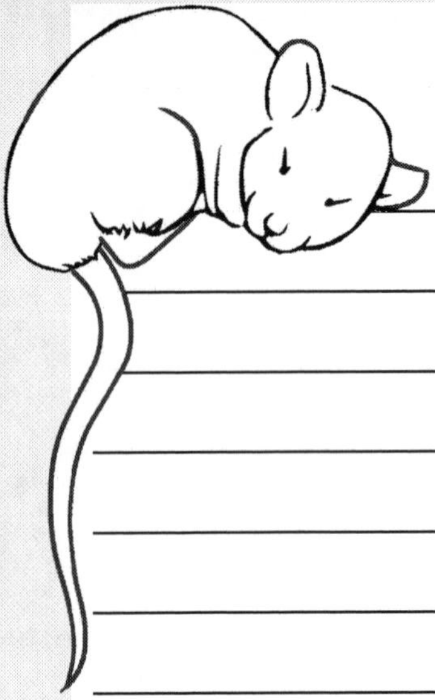

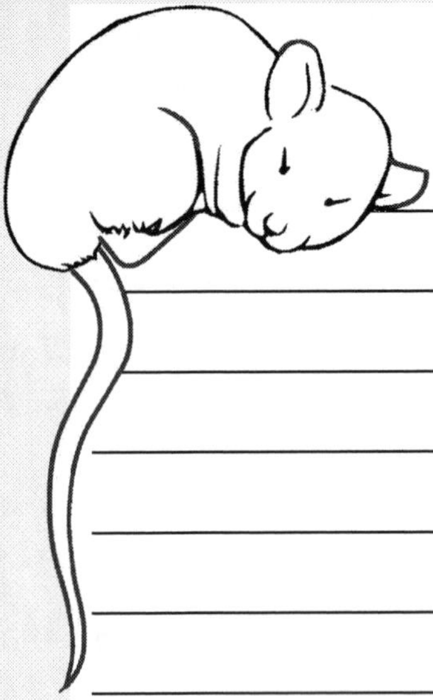

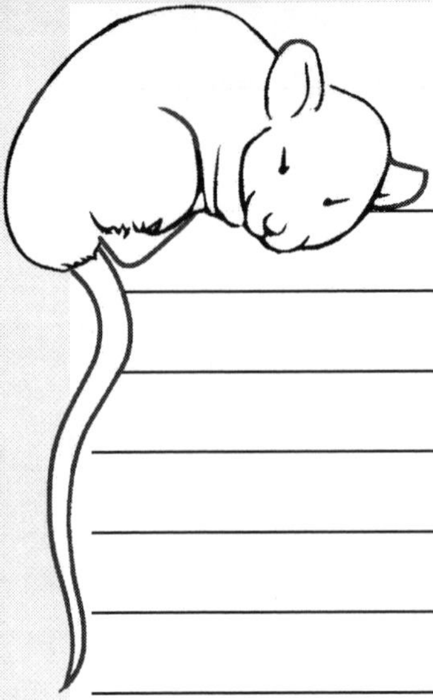

Made in United States
Orlando, FL
27 November 2023

39561178R00061